The Compendium of Lost Poems

by

Caitlin M.S. Buxbaum

Red Sweater Press
P.O. Box 870414
Wasilla, AK 99687
redsweaterpress.com

Copyright © 2019 Caitlin M.S. Buxbaum. All rights reserved.

No part of this book may be used or reproduced in any manner whatsoever without written permission of the publisher except in the case of brief quotations embodied in critical articles and reviews.

Cover image taken by the author.

ISBN-13: 978-1-7332677-4-8
ISBN-10: 1-7332677-4-3

For all the unsung heroes of our time

Contents

SENSES

Shiver	11
Outside on a Tuesday	12
Origins	13
Along the Arroyos	14
At a Choir Concert	15
Lost on Me	16
Perspective	17

SECRETS

After Talking with Two Irishmen I Met in a Bar in Canada	21
Bottled	22
Hidden	23
Just a Friend	24
The Silent Burn	25
September 29, 2013	26
A Wet Spoon	27

RHYTHMS

Thunder Town	31
On a Run	32
The Candy Jar	33
Swing Wide	34
Cross-*Cult*-ural	35
Pastoralis	36

PLACES

Persepolis Illustrated	39
In Reading	40
In difference	41
Shaken Days	42
Blinds	43
Japanese, in Love	44

CHOICES

Trying to Learn English from a Carburetor	47
Writing Genghis Khan	48
Toy Pistol	49
Siren World	50

The Compendium of Lost Poems

SENSES

Shiver
Outside on a Tuesday
Origins
Along the Arroyos
At a Choir Concert
Lost on Me
Perspective

Shiver

It must be the water, I thought,
pelting my skin with the lightness
of a lily brushing by—compared to a
hailstorm, at least. The hotter it gets
the colder the air around me becomes
and is it the droplets sticking to my
epidermal hairs or my thoughts that
are making me shiver?

Outside on a Tuesday

Fifty-seven degrees
Fahrenheit and there's snow
on the ground—not a good day
to be buried.

Origins

A small white feather flown in
on the breeze of passing trucks
winds down and around
a bicycle chain to land at
concrete's feet. From the lint screen
in the dryer a mile away, its brethren
fall to dustier depths inside
a trash can. Maybe origins, then,
mean less than we thought
in the wake of unindividuality.

Along the Arroyos

freesia, lilac, lavender, chop
sewage;
pizza, laundry and flavored
tobacco; then
runner sweat, a biker's bet
that he can pedal faster
than your spinning
legs,
and lungs,
catching breath, catching scents
and sensibility gone   lost

as sight begins
to slumber with the sun
along the arroyos

At a Choir Concert

notes dance above the heads
of unseen singers as their songs
echo upward with a shimmer,
like the exchange of a silver baton
in a 1600-meter relay: sharp,
crucial, ephemeral—if not,
disaster

but, perhaps, wearing maroon
robes burned with age and
experience wards off consequences...

in the sea of pew people,
only I'm thinking
of cassava leaves
and African sun.

running through the snow
lungs louder than legs, bigger
mouths than ideas

Lost on Me

Perspective

A campfire smells different
in November than it does
in June; you might even say
it's a fact of life—but then
again, it could just be me.

SECRETS

After Talking with Two Irishmen I Met in a Bar in Canada
Bottled
Hidden
Just a Friend
The Silent Burn
September 29, 2013
A Wet Spoon

After Talking with Two Irishmen I Met in a Bar in Canada

for Sam & Holmesy

a cat creating static sparks
on a body's pillow at night,
before hunkering down,
reminds me what it's like to be
simultaneously
intrigued, shocked and wary
when handling the simple
things in life;
perhaps such a sensation
is only discovered in those
pre-sleep moments, ever
again unreachable; but

then again,
we've just coaxed the morning into being
with our cultured conversation

Bottled

The bottle
got a hold of his life
after rain and gray sunshine
sold them backpacks
heavy with privilege;
Europe never told them
who controls the inebriated
weather in "Western" society.
So when Harry rang
Sally's bell, and Stockholm
crashed into a stout Irish sea,
adventure told the man
in the long black tie
to kiss the Miller-child's lips —
never again did he
from sleep awaken.

The bottle
got a hold of his life
and sank their ship
with backpacks full
of privilege.

Hidden

A satyr of imitation porcelain
stands guard at the door
of a mumbling house; in the backyard,
a forty-inch rack hangs proudly
above the entrance to a new old tool shed,
governing the sacred gateway,
shielding from untrained eyes.

Inside, a boy bleeds ink
with his new tools
for a lost lover
he can no longer touch —

no one knows.

Just a Friend

No, she's
Just a Friend, you said.
Just, just, just. No, it isn't—you
didn't even give me a chance to
state my case. Or maybe you did
and I missed it; that would be worse.

Just a Friend, only a friend, you said.
Why does anyone want to be a friend
when it's only just, and not right or lawful?
Somebody ruined the dictionary that taught
you words. Or no one told you how to use them.

Just a Friend is a sexless excuse, a Swiss safe haven that
won't hold you responsible for things like emotion
and attachment. But maybe I'm not being fair.
Maybe you really tried to feel it out and
sneak the secrets out of me—secrets

I didn't know I had until you said I'm
Just a Friend. I didn't know what I had
when Justice got confused with a
minimalist. Then again, maybe I
never would without those twin

opposites. It's a miracle language
gets us anywhere at all. I just
thought you'd like to know,
I said. I guess I'm guilty of
oversimplifying, too. But
who exaggerated?

The Silent Burn

Despite the silent burn of one
man's love, alone, she knows she has
the freedom to walk in the sun.

Through window eyes his fingers run;
in fear, clear turns to mirrored glass,
despite her silent burn for One.

In lakes too deep, the image spun
as her reflection drains the past:
the freedom to walk in the sun.

Love not yet old, a new begun:
prima facie, in light will stand,
unlike the silent burn from One.

Soon night dawns black—all's cold and shunned.
Warmth's absence felt, one thought's at hand:
no freedom walks with liars' sons.

Despite love's truth, cruel patience won
the gift of time spent slowly, and
gone is the silent burn from One,
the freedom to walk in the sun.

September 29, 2013

Running my finger over the
callouses on my left hand,
where your ring used to be,
disconcerts me. To see
the physical manifestation
of what once was, lingering
on my soft skin as a hardened
mass not yet disappeared, is
like staring at the bones of
one unredeemed. Will justice
ever be served?

We may never know
the power of our own actions.

A Wet Spoon

Sometimes, reality crushes you like a wet spoon through
pound cake:

>   slowly,
>   heavily,
>   deeply,
>   coldly,

incongruous with what "just makes sense."

Other times, it might be reminiscent of the bitch slap
you wish that girl had given you in seventh grade
so you could hate her:
sharp, but quick,
painful, but final.
Absolute. Resolute. Time to move on.

Today,
you're just wishing
that the banana split plastered on your four-year-old cousin's
face
matters more than making a career
out of words already launched
from the cocoon of originality and the unknown.

Tomorrow,
you'll throw that dishwasher-wet spoon
in the drawer and hope it feeds another happy mouth
before it has a chance
to press its face through the pound cake again.

RHYTHMS

Thunder Town
On a Run
The Candy Jar
Swing Wide
Cross-*Cult*-ural
Pastoralis

Thunder Town

Thunder!
A car door slams.
Thunder!
A baluster bends.
Thunder!
A marching band plays.
Thunder!
A music man sways
to the rhythm and blues
of smooth jazz, dark
as the night behind
closed Negro eyes —
suddenly, I'm caught
in the downpour
of small-town
HighLife
soul.

On a Run

splish, splish, slap, swak
through the February slush
puddles up the sidewalk
next to the trailer park
portables with the black
Bar-B-Q bulb lawn ornament
out front across from the
Assisted Living
who needs help
I can smell someone but
does anyone have a home here?

I do down the road
around the corner on the
hill where there are
thousands of hearts but
sometimes their feet take
them elsewhere —
tuition can't push you out
of house and home like
a social worker can.

The Candy Jar

coffee-table-corner crystal: fragile. uninviting.

destination: inside. objective: a Reese's hidden in the mints and the house of stale Kisses, palmed.

mother: "ask Granma." double intimidation: crystal. fluffy, white age. fragile.

deep breath. Granma? "If it's okay with your mom." permission.

Eight's fingers — delicate — crystal — delicate — hold breath — chocolate. lid secure. exhale.

antiques' breakability: never known so fully as by childish youth.

Swing Wide

Swing wide dearie, swing wide
on the wings of the dawn,
you door to nowhere —
somewhere, perhaps, if only
in dreams yet unawakened.
As it is, your undiscovered potential
lies dormant.

Open to the greatest sea,
open to the highest hill,
open to the mother's womb
and enter in from whence ye came.

Open to the newest moon,
close on the darkest day,
and forever live in dread
of solid faith's decay

but only for a little while,
until the hinges fall free
and down falls the door on its
pure, white face to admit, omit
none, through thee

And whatever may come
And whatever shall pass
the spirit lingers on —
the mind to grass, the body to stone,
swinging wide on the wings of the dawn.

Cross-*Cult*-ural

Today I found
that the month of May,
in Japanese, sounds like
the gentle rap of fingernails
on a stainless steel counter-top,
folding dishrags — *go gatsu...
go gatsu...go gatsu* — and

high society,
like the clack of heels
in an elevator,
the hard-hearted steel immovable
beneath her feet, yet under authority
of democracy; *priv-i-lege —
priv-i-lege — priv-i-lege...*

Taking the elevator backwards
to the laundry room with a cart
full of aprons and dishrags to pay
for school and steel myself against
the *go-getters* rapping their fingernails
against my skull, kicking at my heels,
to *edge* me into The American Way,
privy to democracy, I smile,
and wonder

at my small, stupid rebellion:
diving into the bottomless
writing pool, with a heavy hobby
in Japanese.

Pastoralis

for KJ

If the *passion & purpose*
of a pastor with a sp-peech impediment
can't shake your faith, consider
his parish of perishing honeybees –
beautiful & fragile & deadly –
"programmed to always go
to a better place," *just like people*
provoked by choice, or survival…

What *relevance & risk*
runs so deep in a man's soul,
in a man's *soil*,
that it escapes in his every breath,
reflecting back and about
the mirror of the universe?

May we all unearth
our own inner apiarists
before we meet our final fate.

PLACES

Persepolis Illustrated
In Reading
In difference
Shaken Days
Blinds
Japanese, in Love

Persepolis Illustrated

Behind the curtain you
drink your scotch and
listen to Iron Maiden
to fly
to some place
where God's name
is Ed
or Mary
or Joe;
in the end, even dogs
know when it's time
to die.

In Reading

"There's always room for one more in the crematorium!"
— Smoke Over Birkenau

Folding covers closed, I hear revving
motorcycles in the midst of misery drawn
from the pages of an infamous story (or
on the weary faces of those branded for
destruction), albeit not one often told
on so personal a level

Here, a hundred years in the future,
sunbathing, I sweat and struggle to
summon an appropriate level of
sympathy (and turn a summer scene
into a death camp) but I know it's
impossible

Meanwhile, I look for bruised rain
clouds which inevitably accompany
the record of death. Where hope
feigns residency, I search without
seeing, only thinking, "it's a miracle
we've retained our humanity at all."
Then again,

maybe "American" is merely an
unknowingly idealistic state
of mind in humans who have no
idea of the true state of things
in their own history; only
experience speaks of that which
could be known, but never was.

In difference

I am ashamed to be White
when I see Hollywood productions
of mass murder and genocide —
when theatrical art tells the story
of otherness and oppression as an exposé,
I want to weep and wonder
if I am any different. I committed
no murder and I hated no race,
but what about the love I never
gave, the thoughts I never had
for someone less privileged than I?
How does one go on living
with the sense of belonging to such
a character which causes utter devastation,
one of ignorance and arrogance? Is
to come to terms with the past possible,
for the preservation of the future?

I'm waiting for the answer,
and I wonder
if I am like them.

Shaken Days

> *for Claire*

sweeping slowly, a brown hand
around the wooden handle
of a broom; on the same street,
a chocolate hand in mine
swinging slowly to the rhythm
of our sandals in the sand
with a thousand miles behind us
and a million more to go

when she speaks, I let the Rs and Ws
roll over me as they bounce off her
protruding belly—one year from now
she'll be teaching those letters
to a mouth born of her own flesh

in twenty years, I wonder
if she'll remember the story
I've already misplaced in the mass
of memorialized strangers—
her story of those shaken days.

Blinds

Watching my new mother
close the blinds in the tatami room
is like staring into an aquarium,
long enough to where
I can no longer distinguish
my fingers from the glass walls,
yet I know I am not engulfed
in water; perhaps this means
I am not yet drowning in Japanese
enough to stand in fear of finding
the balance between who I have been
and who I will be. But as quickly
as I've forgotten who, what and where
I am, my mother is walking away
without understanding the grace & beauty
of her actions in my watery eyes.

Japanese, in Love

I wonder what it means
to not burn with passion
in the face of everything
you want. J-drama or no,
the space between two lovers
makes me want to scream,
to ask the questions "why"
and "how" — and after all,
what does it mean to be
Japanese, in love?

CHOICES

Trying to Learn English from a Carburetor
Writing Genghis Khan
Toy Pistol
Siren World

Trying to Learn English from a Carburetor

For an American,
learning a new language without
hearing it aloud
is about as sensible as
trying to learn English
from a carburetor,
for a person of
any other nationality

but at least
for the foreigner, there is
the great possibility of their attempt
going up in smoke — as a result of
mishandled machinery —
to notify them
of their terrible mistake.

Writing Genghis Khan

"you can only have so much stuff
out there on the steppe," Jack said,
telling the story of a boy, not a man,
in love—is this the ancient conqueror
I've heard so much about, or not?

Not herder, nor hunter,
neither Cain, nor Abel, (although
he did kill his half-brother),
his care for his daughters was so great
that the records were censored...

so I wonder: is the Mongol myth
the true history, or the result
of Dr. Weatherford's "middle-aged moment,"
after being served Korean chocolate bars,
little bottles of vodka, and cow tongue
by the Mongolian airlines?

Toy Pistol

I found it in the middle school
parking lot—just an inch long, black
warming on the sunned, April pavement.
Somehow, I could tell that something
had been triggered in a young mind
far too early for the summer
to be safe.

Siren World

    after Cormac McCarthy's The Road

a lovelier song
was hardly ever sung
that deceived so many
of a mind to dream—
perhaps that's why
we writers wander past
the wonder of reality.

Acknowledgments

Thank you to my husband, for putting up with my impatience, for reading through my poems (especially the ones that aren't about him), and for convincing me to take a breath before publishing yet another book. Thank you also to the poets of the internet and the positive ways you've chosen to use social media in sharing your work and appreciating that of others.

About the Author

Caitlin M. S. Buxbaum is a poet, novelist and former journalist from Wasilla, Alaska. She has a Master of Arts in Teaching from the University of Alaska Anchorage and a Bachelor of Arts in Japanese and English with an emphasis in Creative Writing from Gustavus Adolphus College.

Other Books by Caitlin M. S. Buxbaum

Ever Unknown, Ever Misunderstood

Songs from the Underground

Uneven Lanes

Wabi-Sabi World: An Artist's Search

Follow the author on Facebook, Instagram & Twitter @caitbuxbaum or visit her website: caitbuxbaum.com

www.ingramcontent.com/pod-product-compliance
Lightning Source LLC
Chambersburg PA
CBHW070634050426
42450CB00011B/3193